FRANKNESS By Dr. Frank

FRANKNESS
By
Dr. Frank

Self-Awareness Through
Thought Provoking Expressions

Frank J. Brown, III, D.D.S

x

NEW YORK

FRANKNESS By Dr. Frank
Self-Awareness Through Thought Provoking Expressions

ISBN 978-1-61448-279-6 paperback
ISBN 978-1-61448-280-2 eBook
Library of Congress Control Number: 2012935937

Morgan James Publishing
The Entrepreneurial Publisher
5 Penn Plaza, 23rd Floor,
New York City, New York 10001
(212) 655-5470 office • (516) 908-4496 fax
www.MorganJamesPublishing.com

Cover Design by:
Rachel Lopez
www.r2cdesign.com

Interior Design by:
Bonnie Bushman
bonnie@caboodlegraphics.com

In an effort to support local communities, raise awareness and funds, Morgan James Publishing donates a percentage of all book sales for the life of each book to Habitat for Humanity Peninsula and Greater Williamsburg.

Get involved today, visit
www.MorganJamesBuilds.com.

DEDICATION

*This book is dedicated to the
future happiness of mankind.*

HAPPINESS

*Future wife, Pat and I
before my senior prom*

CONTENTS

PREFACE

The following random thoughts and many ole-fashioned clichés are meant to be shared. Most of the quotes originated with the author himself unless listed otherwise. Clichés stand on their own, and I cannot take credit for anything that I did not write. Frankness By Dr. Frank

The Brown's 1st and 2nd Generations

is just plain, old, straight-forward thinking. Read very carefully, because there might be something to focus on. I can in no way apologize for this creation, because some things in our present society need to be brought to light. Frankness is an adjective meaning free, forthright, and sincere expression. FJB3

MOMENTS IN LIFE
(Sharing And Caring)

"Life, be in it."

The Brown's 2nd and 3rd Generations

"You are what you are because of where you were when you were reared. Your childhood influences your adult behavior since your system of values lock in around the ages between ten and twelve."

—*Anonymous*

"Life, live it."

"It's never too late to try and be what you wanted to be."

—*Anonymous*

"When in doubt, check it out."

"You cannot trust just anybody."

"Has common sense been buried?"

"Unwanted advice usually goes nowhere."

"Coping in life requires thoughtfulness."

"Tunnel vision causes one to lose perspective."

"Depth perception is a good thing."

"Always give your best."

"Be your own person."

"Look inside yourself to see yourself."

"You can better understand others by understanding yourself."

"Can you listen before you speak?"

"Life is a precious jewel so don't damage it."

"I'm fired up over cremation."

"Shopping is a recreational sport for women, that doesn't require a mouth guard."

"Your 'heart' and your 'soul' are thoughts that come from your brain. One's inner spirit comes from the brain. It is your ability to think, to reason, to feel, and to touch, to see, to taste, to smell; to hear. Your brain powers your thoughts."

"Listening is far more important than speaking."

"A person goes through a lot in a lifetime."

"Profanity is not a second language."

"Don't always take the easy way out."

"Politics often get in the way of reason."

"A crowd can lead you into unforeseen trouble."

"Don't let Hollywood tell you what to do."

"In life, try to give more than you get."

"Listen to your parents; it's for your own good."

"A good parent will never tell you something that will cause you harm."

"It's better to give than to receive, i.e., teachers, parents, coaches, ministers, fireman, and police officers."

"Give from the heart, and don't expect something in return."

"People who appear silent and don't speak can be disturbing."

"I deplore destructive behavior."

"Perform lots of acts of random kindness."

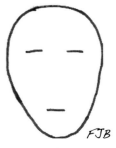

The Blank Stare

"Be a giver, not a taker."

"If you don't want to help, stay out of the way."

"Avoid violence and filth."

"Keep the inside of your car and closet clean."

"Keep sex in the bedroom."

"Life isn't always kind to you."

"Today, many parents are not being parents."

"Your children should be one of your top priorities."

"As parents, you must keep an eye on your children."

"Narcissism is like a horrible disease, sort of a cancer."

"Passive aggression is like pancreatic cancer. It is irreversible."

"Happiness and self-worth come from within and not from the outside."

"Material things can only buy so much."

"The constant acquisition of material objects to try and buy happiness is an endless task."

"Life is what you choose to make it."

"I love southern warmth."

"Some people don't like to be touched and appear to abhor intimacy, while others are huggers, touchers, and kissers; not cold and standoffish."

"Life is about making good choices in order to survive."

"Survival is the name of the game throughout the animal kingdom."

"Acquaintances are not true friends, because they can use you for their own personal gain."

"True friends will stand by you through thick-and-thin."

"Usually one can only have one or two close friends."

"Happiness is like the perception of heaven; it's a state of mind."

"Hollywood is Hollywood."

"Hollywood rarely represents reality."

"Some people lie, cheat, steal, and worse"

"Some people will use you until they can't use you."

"Never put trust in anything but your own intellect; always think for yourself." Linus Pauling

"Life is like a flowing creek. It can start out smoothly, and then suddenly become turbulent before it smooths out again."

"Variety may be the spice of life, but spontaneity spices up life."

"Be true to yourself."

"The sun can shine bright on cloudy days if you imagine that it can."

"Rainy days and Mondays happen."

"Treat people with kindness and they may respond likewise."

"Drunkenness should not be taken lightly."

"Don't let the media sell you down the road."

"Be proactive rather than reactive."

"Tell it like it is."

"Pictures bring things to light."

"All things are not perfect in Camelot."

"Sometimes perfectionism gets in the way of accomplishment."

"I try to stay busy by being busy."

"Sometimes, your best is not good enough."

"If you know what to do, then do it."

"Bigger is not always better, but often it seems so."

"Progress usually comes with consequences."

"Don't follow the crowd, it can lead you astray."

"Make good choices."

"Try to remain calm when things get heated."

"I heard a fellow say that he dropped out of school because school was interfering with what he wanted to do."

PET POEM
"If you can start the day without caffeine,
If you can get going without pep pills,
If you can always be cheerful and ignore aches and pains,
If you can resist complaining and
boring people with your troubles,
If you can eat the same food
everyday and be grateful for it,
If you can understand when your loved
ones are too busy to give you any time,
If you can overlook it when those that love you take it
out on you when, through no fault
of yours, something goes wrong,
If you can take criticism and
blame without resentment,
If you can ignore a friend's limited
education and never correct him,
If you can resist treating a rich
friend better than a poor friend,
If you can face the world without lies and deceit,
If you can conquer tension without medical help,
If you can relax without liquor,

If you can sleep without the aid of drugs,
If you can honestly say that deep in your heart you have
no prejudice against creed, color, religion, or politics;
Then my friend, you are almost as good as your dog."
—*Anonymous*

"It's easy to cling to the past as you get closer to leaving the present."

A THING OF THE PAST

This was one of Norfolk and Western's finest steam locomotives called The 600. I rode in the cab of one of those engines driven by my grandfather, W. C. Montgomery, in 1957.

"Trials and tribulations are called experiences in life."

"Think for yourself and don't let other people think for you."

"A definition of hell: When you think that you are going to die."

"A definition of heaven: When you think that you will live forever."

"Suicide can rob you of your life."

"One-up-man-ship is a distinct form of passive aggression."

"Do you live in disorganized chaos?"

"Do you put things back like you found them?"

"Don't sleep your life away."

"Our lives are not determined by what happens to us but how we react to what happens. Not by what life brings to us, but by the attitude we bring to life. A positive attitude causes a chain reaction of positive thoughts, events, and outcomes. It is a catalyst, a spark that creates extraordinary results."

—*Anonymous*

"Pets can enhance your life."

Warm Love

"I've learned one thing for sure in typing this manuscript. Secretaries earn every penny that they aren't paid for."

"If there were no humans on planet earth, would there still be a God?"

"A person goes through a lot in a lifetime."

"Never do anything that would hurt your parents."

2

DOMESTIC VIOLENCE
(Watch Out)

"There's no excuse for physical abuse."

DOMESTIC VIOLENCE, IT'S ABOUT
CONTROL!

BROKEN GLASS

BROKEN HEART

BROKEN LIFE

FJB

Domestic Violence: It's About Control

"Domestic violence shatters dreams."

"Violence begets violence."

"A restraining order can be a severe false sense of security and lead to your demise."

"Be able to recognize this intimidating threat; if I can't have you than no one else will."

"A downright domestic lie: I'm sorry honey, I'll never do that again."

"A lack of upbringing in the home can contribute to criminal activity."

"Repeat offenders never quit."

"Watch out! Don't become a statistic of domestic violence."

"A domestic violator is a control-freak that uses his/her unacceptable behavior toward another person."

"Born into a home of severe and constant violence, I can speak from years of experience."

"Domestic violators like to deny guilt."

"You intuition can help save your life. If a circumstance doesn't seem quite right at first glance, it probably isn't. Take precaution."

"If you know of someone who has harmed an animal or a pet, you or your friends, and neighbors could be next."

"The best book that I ever read to avoid or to escape from a bad situation is *The Gift of Fear* by Gavin de Becker. Gavin's book offers us survival clues based on our own intuitions that can possibly protect us from violent acts."

"Should you need help with regard to escaping from a threatening situation, you can contact the following:

Gavin de Becker, Incorporated
11684 Ventura Boulevard, Suite 440
Studio City, CA 91604

Or go online to www.gbinc.com or call 1-800-993-6330."

"To report abuse, neglect, or exploitation of a disabled adult or an elderly person, call toll-free 1-800-962-2873."

"Any person, regardless of age, who may be a victim of domestic violence, may call the nationwide Domestic

Violence Hotline at 1-800-799-SAFE (7233) or 1-800-787-3224 (TTY) for immediate assistance."

"Criminals go by there own rules."

"Parents must show interest in their kids."

"What makes people into control-freaks and passive aggressors is mainly their childhood upbringing."

3

BE HEALTHY
(Health Is Better Than Wealth)

"Moderation can be the key to life."

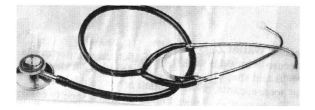

Scope It Out.

"If you have low self-esteem, get in touch with your inner self."

"Learn to see yourself to be yourself."

"A poor lifestyle can do you in."

"Are you food-driven?"

"Do you have an addiction to exercise or to a computer?"

"All drugs are to be used with caution."

"Smoking can be harmful to you and to all other living things."

"The Surgeon General warns that cigars are not a safe alternative to cigarettes."

"Smokeless tobacco is still tobacco."

"It has been said that alcohol is the most lethal drug, outranking heroin, crack cocaine, and marijuana."

"Alcohol is not a cure-all."

"Don't let beer and alcohol take the place of nutrition."

"The constant imbibing of alcohol can ruin anyone."

"Drink to live, not to die."

"Guns can kill within a moments notice."

"Street talk: If I don't win this argument, I'll shoot you dead."

"Obesity can lead to diabetes, heart trouble, stroke, disability, immobility, and death."

"Will you fit into your coffin?"

"How to avoid diabetes? Get a move on!"

"Do you suffer from C.R.S. disease?"

"If it weren't for visits to doctors offices, I would have no social life at all."

"Exercise and recreation are as necessary as reading. I will say rather more necessary, because health is worth more than learning. A strong body makes the mind strong."
—*Thomas Jefferson, 1762 class of William and Mary*

"Thank you for not smoking, pot!"

"You are probably not as crazy as you think you are."

"Often, in the healthcare field, one must treat adults as children and children as adults."

"Make sure that you go to bed with a clean mouth."

FJB

I'll wait and Brush in the Morning.

"I'll do almost anything to avoid a double-chin."

"The father of aerobics, Dr. Kenneth Cooper, said: People don't just die; they kill themselves via a poor lifestyle."

"Take care of yourself 'cause if you don't, no one else will."

"Avoid danger at all cost."

"It's not too late to watch your weight."

"What can make someone moody and/or grouchy or even manic: a lack of food, water, exercise, sleep, money, or a lack of intimacy."

"It's more important how you feel about yourself than what others feel about you."

—*Anonymous*

"Exposed skin can lead to trouble."

"An annual medical physical could pay big dividends and save you money too."

"Do you have Little Hitler's Disease?"

"A kiss and a hug are like a symphony playing."

"Avoid violence."

"Exercise will improve your outlook on life, will increase self-esteem, motivation, your attention-span, and is an aid to sleep."

"Encourage yourself by saying that you can and will do better."

Running With Allen Insley, My Childhood Friend, My Teammate, and my College Roommate

"Your lifestyle can determine your fate."

"Run or walk for health's sake."

"Consistency is hard to beat."

"Exercise increases overall health by improving circulation and brain activity. It sharpens your sight, your taste, hearing, touch, smell, and reduces stress. It makes problems seem smaller."

"When it comes to your health, trust but verify."

"Eat right to be right."

"Time heals some wounds."

"The appearance of your teeth speaks loud of you."

"Sometimes I feel that domestic pets get better care from veterinarians than humans do from physicians."

"After undergoing open-heart surgery, I told the cardiac staff that they were so nice to me that I opened my heart up to them."

"I've had my heart broken before but never like that."

"A.D.H.D. is no fun to play with."

"Information is healthy."

"Sexercise is a pleasant way to lose weight."

"Marijuana, alcohol, and tobacco have helped to ruin many a life."

"Ladies, try to avoid pregnancy by keeping your clothes on."

"I don't have A.D.H.D., so I don't live in a land of fantasy."

"Are you a child in a man's body?"

ENVIRONMENTAL TOPICS
(Be Conservative)

"Over-population with it's subsequent waste products can ruin an ecosystem, i.e., our planet."

Oil Platform

FJB

"Plastic saves lives."

"Knock on formica."

"Wood is often used to provide shelter to people who love trees."

"A larger population increases the risk for crime, pollution, noise, and debt."

"Pollution is a dirty word."

"Oil is necessary to lubricate our society."

"Gasoline provides us with the power to go."

"Water is the universal solvent."

"What's the difference between today's music and noise pollution?"

"Respect your environment; the world is not an ashtray."

"Electricity adds a spark to life."

ON EDUCATION
(This Is It)

FJB

Diploma, a Sign of Progress

"An education is no good unless you know how to use it."

"Education is power."

"Education is a life-long journey; get all that you can."

"Anyone can be a student, but not just anyone can be a student/athlete."

"The pleasure that I obtain from reading is to gain knowledge."

"Get a good education, because it's something that no one can take from you."

"A camera can provide you with a glimpse of the world."

"Photography can open up your eyes."

"When you are trying to teach, you must have a good listener."

"Know how to count, add, multiply, divide, and how to subtract. Know the alphabet and how to spell correctly. Learn to listen so as to learn. This is the basis for education so as to increase your chances for survival."

"If you cannot sign your name so that it can be read, then just sign it with x's."

"You can tune into Sesame Street on PBS to learn your letters and numbers."

"My computer takes me around the world."

"You may not be able to take advantage when opportunity knocks if you aren't educated enough to recognize the opportunity."

"If you don't understand something, ask for help."

"Everyone needs to appreciate the value of an education."

"No matter what degree, diploma, or G.E.D. that you have or don't have, to provide for the most basic needs of food, shelter, and clothing, one must learn early on in life that you need to work. And it wouldn't hurt to have a vehicle, insurance coverage, and gas money."

"The world is a book, and those who do not travel read only one page."

—St. Augustine

ABOUT ATTITUDES
(Improvement Needed)

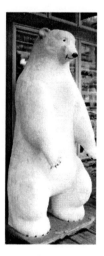

Polar Bear With a Cold Stare

"If you are not smiling, are you happy?"

"If you are smiling, are you happy?"

"Passive aggression has no place on this planet."

"Understanding is a large part of life."

"Imagination can provide you with a different outlook."

"Are you rewarded by making other people miserable."

"Men often only think of themselves."

"The attitudes of some people don't spell success."

"Is this the twenty-first century, where incompetence and ignorance prevail? Or, is it like the 1950's , when there was more reason and good common sense around?"

"Remember, no matter how bad that you think you have it, there's always someone far worse off than you."

"Be nice to people or people won't like you."

"Do you need an attitude adjustment?"

"Are you as neat as you think that you are?"

"People with low self-esteem feel down."

"Being gadget-crazy feeds your ego."

"Social climbers often look down on others."

"The world does not revolve around you."

"Women like to talk, shop, tease, and look pretty."

"Gossip can spread in all directions."

"People with low self-esteem hide behind lousy jokes."

"We can do anything we want if we stick with it long enough."

—Helen Keller

"If your actions inspire others to dream more, to learn, to do more, and to become more, you are a leader."

—John Quincy Adams

"A rainbow can brighten your day."

"Some people have a strange way of showing their appreciation."

"Are you really neat?"

"Lay your butt up in bed all day, and see where that gets you."

"Are you for real or are you just a showboat?"

"Act like you have some sense."

"When hiring a new employee, consider personality over job skills, because skills can be taught; personalities don't change just as a leopard does not change its spots."

THINK POSITIVE

"If you think you are beaten, you are.
If you think you dare not, you don't.
If you'd like to win, but think you can't
It's almost a cinch, you won't.
Life's battles don't always go
to the stronger and faster man.
But soon or late the man who wins
is the one who thinks he can."

—Anonymous

ATTITUDE

"The longer I live, the more I realize the impact of attitude on life. Attitude, to me, is more important than facts. It is more important than the past, than education, than money, than circumstances, than failures, than success, than what other people think or say or do. It is more important than appearance, giftedness or skill. It will make or break a company, a church, a home. The remarkable thing is we have a choice everyday regarding the attitude we will embrace for that day. We cannot change our past. We cannot change the fact that people will act in a certain way. We cannot change the inevitable. The only thing that we can do is play on the one string that we have, and that is our attitude. I am convinced that life is 10% what happens to me and 90% how I react to it. And so it is with you."

—*Charles Swindoll*

"Teenage slogan: I want, I want, and I want!"

"A parent's slogan: Now what have I done?"

"A young person's theme: ME, ME; ME!"

"Never try to be something that you are not."

"I expect songs to tell a story and not just be a lot of noise."

"The general work force demands more than ever before while reluctant to put forth the effort that is needed."

—*Anonymous*

"Sometimes there's just no peace to be had."

"I'm not a know-it-all, so I don't have an opinion on everything."

"Mature adults act like mature adults."

"Slogan for the financial world: Greed is the creed!"

"Let the other person win once-in-a-while."

"I'm more important than you are, and I'm going to make sure that you know it."

"Don't make excuses; let your actions speak for themselves."

"Be considerate of others."

"I'm very positive, I think?"

"Negativity and nagging are close friends."

FASHION ISSUES
(Please Shape Up)

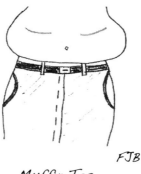

FJB

Muffin Top

"The fashion police: Refers to individuals belonging to an imaginary police force that ensures whether people dress according to good taste or with fashion styles."

"Are you advertising something by the way that you dress?"

"A person usually acts the way that they are dressed."

"To be blond is to brighten your day."

"Are you one of those blond-haired wonders?"

"Do fake blonds get more looks than dyed redheads?"

"The way that you dress affects the way that others see you."

"I've never been in favor of wrinkles of any kind."

"Pretty is as pretty does."

"Do you get enough attention?"

"Tattoos are like keying (scratching) the side of a new car."

"Dress the part; play the part."

"Ladies, are you putting your best front forward?"

"A woman's self-worth is usually based on her appearance."

"Tell me honestly, are you really blond?"

"Don't wear your feelings on your sleeve when you can wear tattoos."

"Don't let someone's appearance fool you."

"What's wrong with looking decent?"

"Cleanliness and orderliness always look better than sloppiness and dirtiness."

"Do you know how to dress as sharp as a tack?"

"Flip-flops are worn often and are often worn out."

"Lady, how is your hair-flicking maneuver working today?"

"Is your vision compromised by your extra-long bangs or are you scared of something?"

"Are men with beards hiding behind something?"

"Many beards come with bald heads."

"Don't tread on loose threads."

"Ladies can you keep your fingers out of your hair?"

"Bright colors can be cheerful, while dark and dull, somber colors impart a feeling of melancholy."

"Why wear black all of the time?"

"Winston Churchill said: I cannot pretend to be impartial about colors and am genuinely sorry for the poor browns."

"Do you call yourself dressed just because you have clothes on."

"Isn't it funny how things wear on you?"

"When you seek attention by the way that you act and/or dress, it's a sign that you need attention."

"Do you look unkept?"

"By the way that you dress, are you an embarrassment to yourself and to civilized society?"

"Your appearance speaks volumes about you."

"Take pride in yourself to be proud of your self."

"Usually, I don't like anything that is fake."

COMMENTS ON
MARRIAGE
(Hidden Love)

"Marriage is not what it's cracked up to be."

Marriage Can Be Topsy-Turvy

"Often a woman thinks more of the diamond on her ring finger than she does of the man that gave it to her."

"Men often give a diamond to get what they want."

"Conditional relationships are suspect."

"Sometimes, in marriage, you aren't allowed to be yourself. You will usually find yourself trying to please or you're in a comprising situation."

"Marriage can be a game of bait-and-switch."

"Often in marriage, there's no time for daddy."

"Interpersonal relationships can end in heartache and/or a debt crisis."

"Women can be extremely manipulative and deceptively deceiving."

"Marriage can ruin a good relationship."

"How do you spell love? M-O-N-E-Y."

"Marriage should always come with a tool kit, because adjustments will have to be made."

"Guys, before you get married be sure of what you're getting into."

"Unconditional love comes with no conditions."

"Love isn't supposed to result in chronic physical or mental harm."

"A controlling relationship is dehumanizing."

"A wife can smother you with love or drive you to distraction."

"It's difficult when you are in first gear, raring to go and your spouse is in reverse."

"Marriage is about giving, tolerating, and enduring."

"Marriage should be like one continual embrace."

"An affectionate marital relationship should be like you're on your fifth date. It should exhibit spontaneous and passionate warmth."

"If the world consisted of no heterosexual relationships and there was no artificial insemination, then the human race could possibly become extinct."

"My wife and I have a dog. Both the dog and I have leashes, but I have the shortest one."

"When in a relationship, agree to disagree to avoid arguing. Don't argue and fight until someone feels that they are right; maybe you're both wrong."

"You never really know someone until you have lived with them."

"Sporadic lovemaking doesn't cut it."

"Happy is the bride that is not expecting."

"Grandma said to her soon-to-be-married granddaughter that if her future husband likes apple pie, make sure that he gets plenty of apple pie."

"No 'apple pie' can cause manic behavior."

"You shouldn't marry a woman and not be close to her."

"The love for your mate should overcome fatigue."

"No intimacy gives me a headache."

"I'd like to be as close to you as I can for as long as I can."

"Sometimes in-laws act like outlaws."

"When you get in the mood, let me know."

"Love me for what I am and not for what I have."

"If you love someone, say it and show it."

"How to hold a marriage together? Be passionate!"

"Men need intimacy like women need lipstick."

"Intimacy can ruffle some feathers."

"Women get married and expect to be treated like queens, yet they won't treat their husbands like kings."

"When I tell people that my wife and I have two poodles, they ask if the dogs sleep with us. I reply that we have twelve feet in the bed."

"My wife and I go out to dinner two nights a week. She goes on Tuesdays and Thursdays, and I go on Wednesdays and Fridays."

—*Anonymous*

"Women like men with money."

"Trinkets are as important to women as watching sports are to men."

"Most men love sports while most women love to shop. Most men like sex, and most women love to shop. Most men enjoy the outdoors while women like to shop indoors."

"Homosexuality is not a choice but a genetic predisposition like a mutation."

"My friend's wife works full-time Monday through Friday, and she doesn't like to have sex the day before she works or the day after."

"My primary-care physician told me that he wanted me to exercise at least three times a week for thirty minutes at a time. I paused, and told him that my wife wouldn't do that."

"A first marriage is referred to as a starter-marriage."

"A single female, with a six year old daughter, told me that she was ready to marry her newfound soul mate. I wonder who was her first soul mate?"

"The marriage contract is a legal entanglement."

"Self-control is not fostered by a lack of intimacy."

"Extreme frustration can be the result of infrequent and inadequate intimacy."

"I often thought that the husband was more important than the house, but I was dead wrong."

"An intimate home is a BIG DEAL."

"Spontaneous lovemaking can help you go far. It provides one with peace-of-mind, enhances sleep, increases productivity, can be a boost to one's energy level and can motivate you to work harder to raise your income."

"Is it true that you get more loving before marriage than afterwards?"

"Drama queens love soap operas."

"Women have the capacity to remember minutia, and they can use it against you later."

"Little or no intimacy is like a sinking ship; it bottoms-out a relationship."

"A lack of interest on your part doesn't mean a lack of interest on my part."

"Often, the wedding event is more important than the actual marriage. It could even be called paradise lost."

"One way to a man's heart is a Ford pickup F-150."

"Another way to a male heart is a Chevy Corvette."

"A 5-carat diamond could be more than a way to a woman's heart, for about thirty minutes."

"Where there's drama, there's usually gossip."

"A garage is a man's cave."

9

SAFETY ISSUES
(Be On Guard)

50cc Yamaha Vino

"When operating a vehicle, signal your intentions long before you execute your intentions."

"Stop means S-T-O-P!"

"Do SUV's hold more than one person?"

"Often nothing much good happens after midnight."

"Say, is that a stop sign or a yield sign?"

"Did your vehicle pass its last inspection, because I noticed that your turn signals don't work?"

"Should I stop or just roll on?"

"Vehicle maintenance is a big safety concern."

"A house doesn't take care of itself; you have to look after it."

"Pyrotechnics are for show; let's keep fire in the fireplace."

"Motorcycles and scooters are vehicles too."

"Potholes give me a sinking feeling."

"Some drivers actually own a driver's license."

"Are loud Harley's really safer?"

"Warning: I stop for stop signs!"

"When turning a vehicle, square your corners to keep from cutting someone off or possibly hitting another vehicle head-on."

"Road rage is the rage."

"I like to snow ski, but I don't like to get in the way of the snowboarders."

"When cruising on top of the water, you need to know what's under the water."

"An automobile can keep you from getting to where you want to go."

10

FICTION VERSES FACT
(Perception)

FJB

Fiction Vs. Fact

"There's a big difference between fiction and fact."

"Fiction doesn't speak the truth."

"Fiction is an exaggeration."

"Documentaries inspire me while fiction leaves me cold."

"Fiction is imagination at work."

"Imagination is good for fiction."

"Fiction can set forth an example."

"Imagination can go far."

"Exaggeration can get out of control."

"I'm not superstitious, but I am scared of ghosts."

"There are three sides to every story: your side, the other side, and the truth."

11

ABOUT FINANCES
(A Necessity)

Crumbled Finances

"America was probably the first country to issue credit so that people could buy things that they didn't need, with money that they didn't have, to impress people that they did not know."

—*Anonymous*

"Money isn't everything."

"Money may not be everything, but it's way ahead of whatever is in second place."

"Does money equal happiness?"

"The more that you have the more that you have to take care of."

"Pay as you go."

"Money you spend early on can catch up with you later on."

"Easy credit isn't easy."

"Don't spend more than you make."

"Are you old enough that your wants won't hurt you?"

"Always put business before pleasure."

"All written contracts should be in one inch high letters with no fine print."

"A lazy lifestyle can leave you short-changed."

"Don't let your wants surpass your needs."

"Money seems to be the basis for much evil."

"Don't let temptation get the best of you."

"10% of all your gross wages should be yours to keep."

"It's not how much that you make but how much that you take care of."

"Always better yourself; never lower yourself."

"Whatever you do in life, if it's not making you money then it's costing you money, and you may need that money when you are not working."

"When you do spend your hard earned money, what have you got to show for it?"

"You can't just live off love. It takes a good income."

"Don't be house poor."

"Watch out for anyone trying to sell you something."

"Shopping is highly skilled entertainment."

"Excessive shopping can land you in the poorhouse."

"A shopping diva: I came, I saw, I spent."

"I'm a single mother with five kids ages six months, two years, three years, four years, five years, and I live fairly well on welfare. My age is 20."

"If it's cute and on 'sale', buy it."

"What the big print giveth, the fine print taketh away."

"Shoppers don't need any encouragement."

"The best things in life are not things."

—Anonymous

"Generally speaking, what most issues come down to is that <u>it's all about money</u>."

"Two rules for frugal shoppers: 1. Don't buy anything unless you need it. 2. Make sure that you need it before you buy it."

"Forget partying, and put work before pleasure if you care to get ahead in life."

"Tight times require tight discipline. Are you up for the challenge?"

"I'm a skateboarder, a snowboarder, and a surfboarder; I do not have time to work."

"If you cannot afford a Porsche, try a Honda S-2000."

Honda S-2000 With License Plate Va. N&WRR in honor of my grandfather, W.C. Montgomery.

"Don't be tempted by temptation."

"Money is hard to earn but easy to spend."

"Don't let money burn a hold in your pocket."

"Credit cards are debt cards; they are not cash."

12

MULTIPLE CLICHES
(Ole Words)

Neither Here Nor There

"Don't practice your mistakes."

"When you assume, you make an ass out of u-and-me."

"All that glitters is not gold."

"There is no such thing as a free lunch."

"Use your head for something besides a hat rack."

"Idle hands; idle mind."

"Life is not fair."

"Haste makes waste."

"Don't be a blight on society, because that costs everybody."

"You'll never mount to a hill-of-beans."

"Clothes can make the man."

"A watched pot never boils."

"Let a sleeping dog lie."

"Curiosity killed the cat."

"Don't play with fire."

"Money talks."

"There is strength in numbers."

"When a shoestring is in a knot, patience will untie it."

"Things are often not what they seem."

"Don't believe everything that you hear, read, or see."

"You're a day late and a dollar short."

"It's my way or the highway."

"You don't miss what you've never had."

"Take care of your tools, and your tools will take care of you."

"Have a place for everything and everything in its place."

"The devil made me do it."

"A lack of planning on your part doesn't constitute an emergency on my part."

"If the shoe fits, wear it."

"Some excuse is better than no excuse."

"The grass is always greener on the other side, especially if it's synthetic turf."

"Age is just a number, but oh what a number."

"Never give up. Never ever give up!" Sir Winston Churchill

"Do you think that money grows on trees?"

"War is hell to people and to all other living things."

H-Bomb

"Stuff happens."

"If momma isn't happy, nobody is happy."

"Quality never costs as much as it saves."

"Locks are for honest people."

"You've made your bed, now lie in it."

"A perfect example of a lack of common sense, someone who can't pour urine out of a boot with the directions written on the heel."

"Have you been so low that you needed an umbrella to keep the ants from wetting on you."

—*Anonymous*

"The old golden-rule: Do unto others as you would have them do unto you. The new golden-rule: Do unto others before they do unto you."

"If you expect to soar with the eagles by day, you can't hoot with the owls all night."

—*Anonymous*

"It was good while it lasted."

"If it feels good, do it."

"If you don't have your health, you don't have anything."

"Think before you leap."

"I may be good, but when I'm bad I'm really good."

"A kind voice is to the heart what light is to the eye. It not only sings but shines."

—Elihu Burritt

"Some people come into our lives and quietly go, while others enter and leave footprints on our heart, and we are never the same."

—Anonymous

"You get what you pay for."

"Think before you act."

"Don't be a fool, go to school."

"For heart health, if it tastes good don't eat it."

"There's no rest for the weary."

"Laughter is the best medicine."

"Some people wouldn't be happy if you gave them a million dollars."

"Discretion is the better part of valor."

"Let bygones be bygones."

"Beggars can't be choosers."

"You don't miss something until you don't have it."

"Don't be penny-wise and pound foolish."

"Don't cry over spilt milk."

"Beauty is only skin deep."

"When in Rome, do as the Roman's do."

"Say what you mean, and mean what you say."

"Life is not all about you."

"Talk to me straight, don't give me a song-and-dance."

"Laugh and the world laughs with you, cry and you cry alone."

"Don't put off tomorrow what you can do today."

"Two is company, three's a crowd."

"The best laid plans of mice and men often go astray."

"The pen is mightier than the sword."

"No news is good news."

"Never underestimate the power of a woman."

"Don't change horses in midstream."

"Strike while the iron is hot."

"Better late than never."

"A bird in-the-hand is worth more than two in the bush."

"You only get out of something what you put into it."

"Children should be seen and not heard."

"There are none so blind as those who cannot see."

"You can lead a horse to water, but you can't make it drink."

"Two wrongs don't make a right."

"Don't look a gift horse in the mouth."

"You reap what you sow."

"It's just salt in the wound."

"Speed kills."

"A boat is a hole in the water that you pour money into."

"Keep your nose out of other people's business to keep from getting your head bitten off."

"Save for a rainy day."

"Nothing beats a trial but a failure."

"If at first you don't succeed, try and try again."

"Justice has it's own reward."

"Never say never."

"Don't interfere with a working man."

"Practice what you preach."

"Agree to disagree."

"Misery loves company."

"Give credit where credit is due."

"Get down-to-earth."

"Sometimes you have to go around your elbow to get to your thumb."

"At times, the right hand doesn't know what the left hand is doing."

FOUR OF DR. BROWN'S
FAVORITE VERSES
(Golden Words)

HAVE YOU EARNED ONE MORE TOMORROW?

"Is anyone happier because
you passed his way?
Does anyone remember that
you spoke to him today?
Were you selfish, pure and simple,
as you rushed along your way?
Or is someone mighty grateful
for a deed you did today?
Can you say tonight in parting
with the day that's slipping fast,
That you helped a single person
in the many that you passed?
Is a single heart rejoicing
over what you did or said?
Does someone whose hopes were
fading now with courage look ahead?
Did you waste the day or lose it?
Was it well or poorly spent?
Did you leave a trail of kindness
or a scar of discontent?
As you close your eyes in slumber
do you think that one might say,
"You have earned one more tomorrow
by the work you did today?"

—Anonymous

THE BUTTERFLY

"The butterfly is only on earth for a very short time, but it goes from flower to flower taking pollen from one and spreading it to another, helping to make the world more beautiful after it is gone than before it came."

—*Anonymous*

A SMILE

"A smile costs nothing but gives much.
It enriches those who receive
Without making poorer those who give.
It takes but a moment.
But the memory of it sometimes
Lasts forever.
None is so rich or mighty that
He can get along without it.
And none is so poor but that
He can be made rich by it.
A smile creates happiness in the home,
Fosters good will in business,
And is the countersign of friendship.
It brings rest to the weary.
Cheer to the discouraged,

Sunshine to the sad and it is nature's
Best antidote for trouble.
Yet, it cannot be bought, begged,
Borrowed, or stolen, for it is
Something of no value
To anyone until it is given away.
Some people are too tired to give you a smile.
Give them one of yours
As none needs a smile
So much as he who has no more to give."
—*Genny Anderson*

OLD FOLKS

"Remember Old Folks are worth a fortune, with silver in their hair, gold in their teeth, stones in their kidneys, lead in their feet, and gas in their stomachs. I have become a little older since I saw you last, and a few changes have come into my life since then. Frankly, I have become quite a frivolous old gal. I am seeing five gentlemen every day. As soon as I wake up, Will Power gets me out of bed. Then, I go see John. Then, Charlie Horse comes along, and when he is here he takes a lot of my time and attention. When he leaves, Arthur Ritis shows up and stays the rest of the day. He doesn't like to stay in one place very long, so he takes me from joint to joint. After such a busy day, I'm really tired and glad to go to bed with Ben Gay. What a life!

P.S. The preacher came to call the other day. He said at my age I should be thinking about the hereafter. I told him, oh, I do all the time. No matter where I am, in the parlor, upstairs, in the kitchen, or down in the basement. I ask myself, now....... "What am I here after?"

—Anonymous

ABOUT THE AUTHOR

Graduation Three

Frank Johnson Brown, III was born on March 15, 1942 in Newport News, Virginia. He is a 1960 graduate of Warwick High School, a 1964 graduate of The College of William and Mary, and a 1968 grad of The Medical College of Virginia School Of Dentistry. He retired from his private dental practice after serving in his hometown for close to forty years.

In 1960, he received a four-year athletic grant-in-aid to William and Mary for his abilities in the sport of track. He was also recruited by Furman University, Randolph-

Macon College, and by Wake Forest University. He was the 1960 Group AAA Virginia State Champion in the one-mile run, the winner of the Virginia State Junior A.A.U. one-mile run that same year, and the 1961 State Intercollegiate freshman indoor champ in the half-mile and the one-mile runs. He ran cross-country, indoor and outdoor track throughout all four years in college while pursuing a rigid pre-dental degree. He was captain of the 1963 victorious Southern Conference cross-country team that competed in the N.C.A.A. Championships held at Michigan State University. In 1990, he was inducted into The City of Newport News' High School Track and Field Hall of Fame; stating at that time that some hall was better than no hall.

Dr. Frank's
Retirement Announcement

Fulfillment

"I want to thank all the kind patients that gave me a chance to serve them. You enriched my life beyond my fondest dreams!"

—Frank J. Brown, III, D.D.S.

POSTSCRIPT:
Overcoming Adversity

Born into a marriage of severe and constant domestic violence, I endured that awful situation until I too was married twenty-four years later. Did okay in grade school, and did well academically throughout high school. I deeply wanted to earn an athletic letter in high school. So, I tried out five times for various athletic teams only to be cut due to a noticeable lack of ability in those sports. However, I always believed in myself, had lots of quite self-confidence, and much determination to succeed in life. I then went out for the high school track team in November of my junior year. Low-and-behold, I had found my niche; I could run like crazy. I was quiet, shy, and introverted, but oh could I run; and run I did. Being an extremely hard worker with an excellent coach, by the name of Jim Hubbard, I quickly reached immediate rewards that I never dreamed possible. After only sixteen months of varsity competition,

I had earned all-state honors in cross-country, indoor, and outdoor track in four different events as a middle-distance runner.

Though I was never even remotely prepared for any S.A.T tests, I was accepted into the college of my choice on an athletic scholarship. But, upon acceptance I was empathetically told by the Dean of Admissions that, based on my poor S.A.T scores, he would let me in but that I would never graduate. Whereupon, I remarked to myself that I had not flunked out yet; so let's get started.

Coach Jim Hubbard at Warwick

I graduated in four years after completing an arduous pre-med curriculum. Plus, I was on eight intercollegiate state championship teams and on two winning Southern Conference teams in my favorite sport. Yes, I did it the hard way, and managed to overcome adversity again. I then went on to graduate from dental school.

Eighteen years later, I was mysteriously diagnosed with a medical anomaly that, without explanation and without proper follow-up, resulted in my being placed on several intense medications that slowly took my health down over the next twenty-three years. After some near-death experiences, I became my own advocate only to discover two years later that I was suffering from damage to my heart and kidneys. Now, after finding a magnificent nephrologist and a knowledgeable cardiologist and undergoing open-heart surgery, I find myself on another uphill fight. So, I say: Never ever give up! This is *Frankness* by Frank.

CPSIA information can be obtained at www.ICGtesting.com
Printed in the USA
BVOW07085429081 2

299062BV00001B/3/P